The Art of Engagement

How to Speak Persuasively and Captivate Any Audience.

Henry Scott. Jnr

Table of Contents

Introduction

The Art of Engagement

Are you looking to become an effective and powerful public speaker? Have you been searching for a comprehensive guide that can help you master the art of public speaking? Whether you are a student, a business professional, or any other individual wanting to sharpen their communication skills, this book is for you.

In this book, "The Art of Engagement: How to Speak Persuasively and Captivate Any Audience," you will learn the essential strategies for successful public speaking. You will discover how to effectively craft your message, engage your audience, and make an impact with your delivery. You will also learn how to overcome your fear of public speaking and make your voice heard.

You will gain insight from experts in the fields of communication and public speaking, who will provide you with actionable advice and resources to help you take the next step in your public speaking journey. With their guidance, you will be able to master the art of public speaking and deliver powerful presentations that will leave a lasting impression.

So, if you are ready to make a difference in your communication skills, then this book is for you. With the right guidance and practice, you can learn to speak with confidence and captivate any.

Chapter 1

Establishing Your Presence: Techniques for Becoming an Engaging Speaker

Establishing your presence as an engaging speaker can be a daunting task. It requires skill, confidence, and persistence. Whether you're delivering a keynote speech or leading a workshop, it's important to be able to engage your audience in order to convey your message effectively. Here are some techniques for becoming an engaging speaker:

1. **Prepare thoroughly**: Preparation is key to any successful presentation. Make sure to research your topics thoroughly and practice your delivery in advance. This will help you be more confident and better prepared to handle any surprises that may arise during your presentation.

2. Get to know your audience: Gather information about your audience beforehand, so you can tailor your presentation to their needs and interests. This will help you capture their attention and make your presentation more engaging.

3. Use visual aids: Visual aids can be a great way to make your presentation more interesting and engaging. Use images, charts, videos, or other visuals to help convey your message and keep your audience's attention.

4. Be dynamic: As much as possible, try to be dynamic in your delivery. Use gestures, vary the tone of your voice, and move around the stage. This will help keep your audience engaged and focused.

5. Use humor: Humor can be a great way to keep your audience entertained and engaged. Just make sure your jokes are appropriate for the audience and the occasion.

6. Involve the audience: Involving your audience in your presentation is a great way to keep them engaged and interested. Ask questions, solicit feedback, and involve the audience in activities or discussions.

7. Be passionate: Show your enthusiasm and passion for the topic. This will help your audience connect with you and be more engaged in the presentation.

These are just some of the techniques for becoming an engaging speaker. With the right preparation and practice, you can become a successful and engaging speaker. Good luck!

Chapter 2

Crafting Your Message: How to Structure Your Speech to Maximize Impact

Having a great speech is essential for any occasion, from a presentation to a wedding toast. Crafting your message is the first and most important step in ensuring that your speech is effective and powerful. Here are some tips on how to structure your speech to maximize its impact.

First, decide on the main message you want to convey in your speech. This will help you structure your speech and make sure that all the points you make support this main idea. Make sure the message is clear and easy to understand, as well as inspiring and motivating.

Next, create an outline for your speech. This will help you organize your thoughts and ensure that your speech is coherent and well-structured. Begin by introducing the topic, then move onto the main body of your speech, and finally, conclude with a powerful ending.

When crafting your message, it is important to use storytelling to make your points. Stories help you connect with your audience and make your points more memorable. You should also use visuals, such as slides or videos, to illustrate your points.

Make sure to use language that is appropriate for your audience. For example, if you are speaking to a room full of business professionals, you should use more formal language than if you were speaking to a group of friends.

Finally, practice your speech multiple times before delivering it. This will help you become more comfortable with the material and ensure that your presentation is polished and professional. Remember to speak slowly, enunciate clearly, and pause for dramatic effect.

Crafting your message is the key to making sure your speech is effective and engaging, so be sure to put in the time and effort to get it right.

Chapter 3

Engaging Your Audience: Strategies for Connecting to Your Listeners

Engaging your audience is essential to the success of any event or presentation. Whether you're giving a lecture, hosting a webinar, running a meeting, or delivering a keynote speech, connecting with your listeners is key to creating a memorable experience. Here are some strategies for engaging your audience and making sure your message hits home.

1. **Know your audience**. Before you can truly engage your audience, you must understand them. Understand who they are, what they care about, and why they're there. This will help you tailor your content to

their interests and create a more meaningful experience.

2. **Make it interactive**. People are more likely to stay engaged if they feel like they're part of the conversation. Use polls, surveys, and other interactive activities to involve your audience and make them feel like their opinions matter.

3. **Keep it conversational**. Don't just lecture your audience – instead, make it a conversation. Ask questions, create a dialogue, and invite your listeners to share their experiences and perspectives. This will help make your presentation more engaging and memorable.

4. **Tell stories**. People love stories and they're a great way to engage your audience. Tell stories that relate to your topic and make your points in a memorable way.

5. Use visuals. Visuals are a great way to add interest and engagement to your presentation. Use slides, videos, diagrams, photos, and other visuals to illustrate your points and keep your audience's attention.

6. Encourage participation. Invite your audience to ask questions, give feedback, and participate in activities. This will help keep them engaged and make them feel like they're part of the conversation.

7. Be passionate. When you're passionate about your topic, it's contagious. Show your enthusiasm and let it shine through your presentation. This will help your audience connect with your message and stay engaged.

Engaging your audience is essential for any successful event or presentation.

By understanding your audience, making it interactive, keeping it conversational, telling stories, using visuals, and encouraging participation, you can ensure that your message resonates with your listeners.

With the right strategies and approach, you can connect with your audience and ensure that your presentation is a success.

Chapter 4

Delivering Your Presentation: Tips for Overcoming Nerves and Connecting with Your Audience

Delivering a presentation can be a nerve-wracking experience. Whether you are giving a speech at a conference, introducing a new product, or simply giving an update, it's important to remain calm and connected with your audience. Fortunately, there are several tips you can use to help you overcome your nerves and make a positive connection with your audience.

1. Take a deep breath and relax.

Before you begin speaking, take a few deep breaths to relax and center yourself. This will help to reduce your stress and anxiety levels and make it easier to focus on the task at hand.

2. **Speak slowly and clearly**. When delivering your presentation, it's important to speak slowly and clearly. This will not only help you to remember what you want to say, but also ensure that your audience can understand you.

3. **Make eye contact.** Making eye contact with your audience will help to create a connection and make them feel more engaged with your presentation.

4. **Use positive body language**. Your body language can have a huge impact on how your audience perceives you. Ensure that you stand up straight and maintain good posture, smile often, and use your hands to emphasize points.

5. Utilize visual aids. Using visual aids such as PowerPoint slides, graphics, and videos can help to make your presentation more engaging and easier to understand.

6. Prepare your presentation thoroughly. Preparing your presentation thoroughly is essential to its success. Make sure you've gone over your presentation multiple times and are familiar with the material.

7. Practice, practice, practice. The more you practice, the more confident you'll feel. Practicing will also help you to identify any potential issues or areas of confusion.

Being prepared, comfortable with the material, and confident in your delivery will help ensure your presentation is a success.

Chapter 5

Analyzing Your Performance: Evaluating Your Delivery and Impact

As a public speaker, it's important to take the time to analyze your performance after each presentation. Taking the time to review your performance and impact can help you become a more effective public speaker and set yourself up for success in the future. This book will provide an in-depth look at what it takes to analyze your performance and evaluate your delivery and impact.

Evaluating Your Delivery: The first step in analyzing your performance is evaluating your delivery. There are several aspects to consider when assessing your delivery, including your use of body language, vocal variety and tone, and storytelling.

1.Body Language. Body language is a key element of any presentation and can have a significant impact on your audience. When evaluating your delivery, consider how you used body language to engage with your audience. Were you able to make eye contact with your audience? Did you use gestures and facial expressions to illustrate your points? How did the audience respond to your body language?

2. Vocal Variety and Tone. Your vocal variety and tone can also have a significant impact on your audience. When evaluating your delivery, consider how you used your voice to engage with your audience. Did you vary your pitch to keep your audience engaged? Did you use a conversational tone to make your points? How did the audience respond to your vocal variety and tone?

3. Storytelling. Storytelling is a powerful tool for connecting with your audience and can be a great way to illustrate your points.

When evaluating your delivery, consider how you used storytelling to engage with your audience. Did you use stories to illustrate your points? Did you use stories to create an emotional connection with your audience? How did the audience respond to your storytelling?

4. Evaluating Your Impact. The second step in analyzing your performance is evaluating your impact. When assessing your impact, consider the reactions of your audience and the feedback you received.

First, consider the reactions of your audience.
Did your audience appear engaged?
Did they have questions or make comments during or after your presentation?
Did they appear to understand the material?

Second, consider the feedback you received.
Did you get positive feedback?

Did you get any constructive criticism? What did you learn from the feedback? Did it help you improve your presentation?

Analyzing your performance is an important part of becoming an effective public speaker. Taking the time to evaluate your delivery and impact can help you become a more effective speaker and set yourself.

Chapter 6

Leveraging Technology: Utilizing Digital Tools for Enhanced Engagement

In today's digital world, leveraging technology is essential for success. Technology can help businesses keep up with the ever-changing marketplace and stay ahead of their competition. By utilizing digital tools, companies can enhance the engagement with their customers, increase productivity, and open up a greater range of opportunities.

One of the most effective ways to leverage technology for enhanced engagement is through the use of social media. Social media platforms allow businesses to reach a wide audience, interact with customers, and share products and services. By creating engaging content and responding to customer inquiries, businesses can create a meaningful connection with their target audience. Additionally, businesses can use social media to track and analyze customer feedback, enabling them to quickly identify potential issues and make any necessary changes.

Another way to leverage technology for enhanced engagement is through the use of data analytics. By collecting data from customers, businesses can gain valuable insights into customer behavior and preferences. This information can be used to create targeted marketing campaigns, develop new products and services, and optimize existing ones. Additionally, data analytics can be used to track customer engagement, providing valuable feedback and allowing businesses to adjust their strategies accordingly.

Finally, leveraging technology can be used to create a more interactive customer experience. For example, businesses can use virtual reality and augmented reality to create immersive experiences for customers. Additionally, businesses can use AI-driven chatbots and voice assistants to provide personalized customer service. By utilizing these technologies, businesses can engage with customers in a more meaningful way and create a more enjoyable experience.

In conclusion, leveraging technology is essential for businesses looking to stay ahead of the competition and increase engagement with customers. By utilizing digital tools such as social media, data analytics, and interactive experiences, businesses can create a more meaningful connection with their target audience and open up a greater range of opportunities.

Chapter 7

Adapting for Different Audiences: How to Tailor Your Message for Different Groups

Whether you're speaking to a large crowd or a small group, it's essential to be able to tailor your message to different audiences. Adapting your message to different audiences is an important skill to master in order to ensure your message is heard and understood.

The key to successful communication is understanding the different needs, interests, and backgrounds of your audience. It's important to think about how to adapt your message to make sure it resonates with each group. Here are some tips for tailoring your message for different audiences.

1. Research the audience: Before you deliver your message, take the time to research your audience. This will help you understand their needs and interests, so you can tailor your message accordingly.

2. Choose the right language: Different audiences respond to different language. Choose your words carefully, to ensure your message is understood.

3. Get creative: Different audiences often respond better to creative approaches. Think about incorporating visuals, audio, or interactive elements into your presentation to engage your audience.

4. Adapt your delivery: Different audiences have different expectations and preferences when it comes to delivery.

Consider tailoring your tone, pace, and volume to suit the audience.

By taking the time to understand your audience and adapting your message accordingly, you'll be able to reach more people, and ensure your message is heard. With the right approach and a bit of effort, you'll be able to successfully tailor your message for different audiences.

Chapter 8

Overcoming Challenges: Dealing with Difficult Questions and Controversial Topics

We all face challenges in life, both in our personal and professional lives. One of the most difficult challenges is dealing with difficult questions and controversial topics. It can be intimidating to face tough questions, especially when the answers may be unpopular or controversial.

However, there are ways to handle difficult questions and controversial topics in a way that is respectful, professional and informative. Here are some tips for overcoming this challenge:

1. **Be prepared**. The best way to approach difficult questions and controversial topics

is to be prepared. Research the topic thoroughly, and consider different perspectives and potential questions. This can help you stay informed and knowledgeable, and will give you confidence when responding.

2. **Stay calm**. It's natural to feel anxious or intimidated when facing difficult questions and controversial topics, but staying calm is essential. Take a few deep breaths, and remember that you are prepared and capable of responding thoughtfully and knowledgeably.

3. **Listen carefully**. It's important to listen carefully to the question, and make sure you understand what is being asked. If you need clarification, ask for it.

4. **Think before you speak**. Before responding to a difficult question or controversial topic, take a few moments to

think about what you want to say. This will help you craft a well-thought-out response.

5. Be Respectful. Even if you disagree with the question or topic, it's important to remain respectful. Avoid personal attacks or emotional language, and stay focused on the facts.

6. Stay on point. Difficult questions and controversial topics can be distracting, so it's important to stay on point. Make sure your response is focused and relevant to the question or topic.

7. Follow up. After responding to the question or topic, take a few moments to follow up and make sure the other person understands your response.

Dealing with difficult questions and controversial topics can be intimidating, but it is possible to overcome this challenge.

Chapter 9

Practicing Your Craft: Strategies for Deliberate Practice and Improvement

The saying "practice makes perfect" is certainly true when it comes to honing a craft. Whether you are a musician, athlete, or writer, it is important to practice regularly in order to stay sharp and improve your skills. Deliberate practice is a method of practice that is focused, structured, and systematic, and it can help you reach your goals faster. Here are some strategies for deliberate practice and improvement.

1.Set Goals: Before you can practice your craft, it's important to set goals. What do you want to accomplish? How will you measure your progress? When do you want to reach your goals? By setting goals, you can create a plan of action and use it to track your progress.

2.Break Down Skills: Once you've set your goals, you need to break down the skills and techniques needed to achieve them. For example, if you're a musician, you might need to learn certain scales, chords, and techniques. By breaking down the skills, you can focus on mastering each one.

3.Focus on Improvement: While practicing, focus on what needs improvement. Don't just go through the motions; be aware of what you're doing and actively work to improve. Identify the areas where you're struggling and work to correct them.

4.Keep Track of Progress: As you practice, keep track of your progress. Note the areas where you're making progress and the areas where you're still struggling. This will help you stay motivated and focused as you work towards your goals.

5.Get Feedback: As you practice, be sure to get feedback from experienced professionals or mentors. They can provide valuable insight and help you identify areas that need improvement.

6.Challenge Yourself: As you practice, challenge yourself. Don't be afraid to push yourself and try something new. By doing so, you'll be able to expand your skills and grow as a great speaker.

Practicing your craft takes time and effort, but it can be a rewarding experience.

Chapter 10

Becoming an Expert: How to Develop Your Public Speaking Skills and Grow Your Brand

Public speaking is an incredibly important skill that can help you to grow your brand and become an expert. Whether you're giving a presentation at work, speaking at a conference, or simply speaking up in group conversations, having strong public speaking skills can help you to stand out from the crowd and make a positive impression.

The good news is that public speaking skills can be developed with practice and dedication. Here are some tips to help you start developing your public speaking skills and grow your brand.

Practice: The key to becoming a good public speaker is practice. Make sure you practice your presentation as much as possible before delivering it. You should also practice speaking in front of a mirror or an audience of friends and family to get feedback and improve your performance.

Be Confident: It's essential that you feel confident when delivering your presentation. If you feel nervous or anxious, take a few moments to take some deep breaths and remind yourself that you can do this.

Be Prepared: Make sure you have all the necessary materials for your presentation and make sure you are familiar with them so that you can explain them confidently.

Use Visual Aids: Visual aids can help to engage your audience and make your presentation more memorable. Try to use illustrations, diagrams, and photos to make your points.

Speak Clearly: Speak in a clear and strong voice and make sure you enunciate your words. This will help your audience to understand you and make sure they are paying attention.

Be Engaging: Make sure you are engaging with your audience by making eye contact, using humor, and asking relevant questions.

Use Body Language: Use your body language to express your points and show your audience that you are confident and passionate about your topic.

By following these tips, you can start to develop your public speaking skills and grow your brand. With practice, dedication and the right attitude, you can become an expert public speaker in no time.

Summary & Conclusion

Summary: This comprehensive guide covers everything about becoming an effective public speaker, from establishing your presence and crafting a message, to connecting with your audience and overcoming challenges. You'll learn tips for delivering your presentation, analyzing your performance, leveraging technology, adapting for different audiences, and practicing your craft. You'll also discover how to become an expert public speaker and grow your brand.

Conclusion: Public speaking is an essential skill to have, and this guide will help you take your skills to the next level. With the techniques outlined, you'll be able to engage your audience, deliver your message with confidence, and build your brand. Developing your public speaking skills will open up new opportunities and help you become a successful speaker.

www.ingramcontent.com/pod-product-compliance
Lightning Source LLC
LaVergne TN
LVHW052110160826
845678LV00015B/3475